Komodo Dragons For Kids

Amazing Animal Books for Young Readers

by Lisa Barry

Mendon Cottage Books

JD-Biz Publishing

Download Free Books!

http://MendonCottageBooks.com

All Rights Reserved.
No part of this publication may be reproduced in any form or by any means, including scanning, photocopying, or otherwise without prior written permission from JD-Biz Corp and
http://AmazingAnimalBooks.com. Copyright © 2015
All Images Licensed by Fotolia and 123RF

Read More Amazing Animal Books

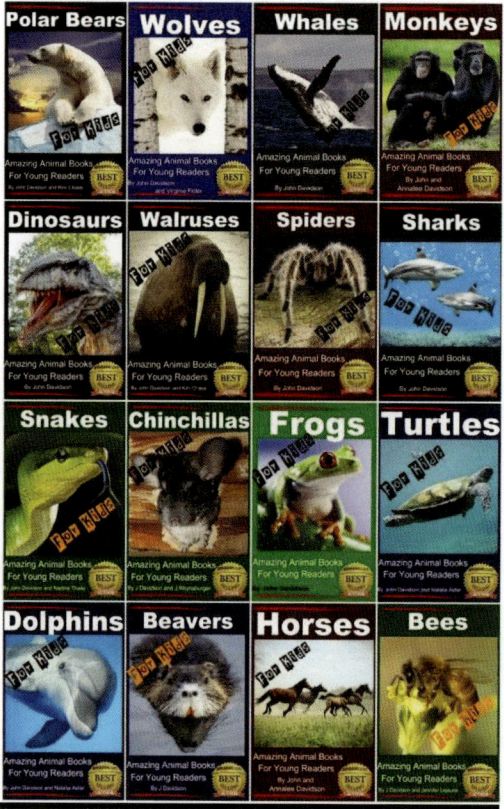

Download Free Books!

http://MendonCottageBooks.com

Table of Contents

1. Komodo Dragon Facts
2. What is a Komodo Dragon?
3. What Do Komodo Dragons Look Like?
4. Where Do Komodo Dragons Live?
5. The Komodo Dragon Home
6. The Komodo Dragons Senses.
7. What Do Komodo Dragons Eat?
8. What Eats the Komodo Dragon?
9. The Komodo Dragon Family
10. Komodo Dragons in Captivity
11. Why are Komodo Dragons Vulnerable?
12. When Komodo Dragons Attack
13. Can I keep a Komodo Dragon as a Pet?

Komodo Dragon Facts

- Komodo dragons are also known as Varanus Komodoensis, komodo monitor, the komodo island monitor, blawak rakasa (this means giant monitor) or ora buaya darat (this means land crocodile)
- Komodo dragons are large lizards.
- Lizards are a type of animal called a reptile.
- Komodo dragons do not breathe fire like the dragons in story books.
- They are the largest living species of lizard.

- They were officially discovered by western scientists in 1910.
- They are classified as vulnerable which means that they are at risk of extinction.
- The biggest ever recorded komodo dragon in the wild was 10ft long (3.13 meters) and weighed 370 lb (166 kg)
- Their size has been called island gigantism by scientists. Many believe that the komodo dragon has become so big because there are no other predators where they live and they have their pick of prey.

- Other scientists feel that the size of the komodo dragon shows a direct link between them and their ancestors; the varanid lizards. These extinct creatures once lived in Australia and Indonesia.
- When a komodo dragon in a zoo needs a blood test, two zoo keepers have to hold it down because it is so powerful, and it does not like blood tests!
- It can run up to 15mph.
- A komodo dragon will attack animals bigger than itself. No other lizard will do this.
- A komodo dragon will keep growing new teeth to replace those that have fallen off or broken while eating.
- Its saliva is poisonous.
- In 2011 Komodo was included in the "New 7 Wonders of Nature" list.
- Komodo dragons are carnivores.
- 3 stuffed komodo dragons can be still seen today in the American Museum of Natural History. They were brought back from an expedition to the Indonesian Islands in 1926 by Douglas Burden.
- Burden also brought back 2 live komodo dragons that were put in a show where people paid a lot of money to see these dragons tied up on a stage. This would never happen today because people would say it was cruel. It was this show that inspired the movie makers to create a famous old film called King Kong from 1933. (it was later remade in 2005) This is about a giant gorilla that is taken from its home and put in a show in America. In the film King Kong escapes from the show to wreak havoc in New York City. The komodo dragons never did that.

What is a Komodo Dragon?

A komodo dragon is a lizard. A lizard is a type of reptile, but what is a reptile?

Cold blood	A reptile is a cold blooded animal. This means its temperature changes with the environment. We are mammals, and mammal's temperature stays the same all of the time, even though we feel hot or cold our core temperature doesn't change. If it changes it is an indication of sickness. If a reptile gets too cold it can literally warm up its body by lying in the sun, if it's too cold, it can dip into cool waters.
Scaly skin	All reptiles have scales to protect their body. These scales can be very different depending on the animal. They can be soft, hard big or small but always scaly.
Eggs	All reptiles are born from eggs that are on land. All reptile mothers leave their eggs after they have laid them and leave their babies to fend for themselves. Because of this reptiles must be born with great instincts so they know what to do without being shown or told.

Other reptiles include crocodiles and snakes.

What do Komodo Dragons Look Like?

- An average komodo dragon adult male can weigh about 150lb (70kg). A small adult human can weigh the same.
- An average komodo dragon adult male will grow to about 85 ft long (3 meters).This is roughly the same length as a small car.
- An average komodo dragon female will weigh a little less and be a little shorter.
- The komodo dragons' tail is very long. In fact it is the same size as its entire body.
- A komodo dragon has teeth that are serrated. This means they have little edges like a bread knife. These are designed to tear flesh.
- A komodo dragon has 60 teeth, many more than an adult human, who has only 32. Each of these komodo teeth can grow up to one inch (25cm)
- A komodo dragon has a long tongue which is yellow. It has an end that splits into two. This is called a forked tongue.

- A komodo dragon has scaly skin. It is strong like chain mail armor that knights used to wear. It is made strong because it has little bones within it called osteoderms. Other lizards, such as crocodiles, are killed for their skin to make into leather products. Luckily for the komodo dragon its skin so rough and tough people generally don't want to use it for leather.

Where Do Komodo Dragons Live?

The komodo dragon is found on a group of Indonesian islands. There are 17,508 islands in total. All together they are called the Republic of Indonesia. The komodo dragon is only found on the following islands…

- Komodo Island,
- Rinca Island,
- Flores Island,
- Gill Motang Island,

The islands are in South East Asia. There are now 2000 people who live on the main Komodo Island. They are decedents of criminals who were sent there many years ago as a punishment. The island is also famous for one of its beaches which has pink sand. These islands form part of the Komodo National Park. People visit the area today primarily for diving in the lush warm waters surrounding the islands.

The islands are tropical. This means that they are hot and can be very wet. They have a high level of humidity which is water in the atmosphere. The islands are affected very little by the seasons. It doesn't get much hotter in the summer or much colder in the winter. The shortest day and the longest day of the year only differ by 48 minutes. This is why the people who live on the islands can grow crops all year round and are not dictated to by the seasons like farmers in most other countries.

Other animals that live on the islands are;

- Buffalo

- Civets
- Cockatoo
- Macaques

The island with the dragon's namesake Komodo is where the creature gets its name from. This is because that is where it was discovered. Stories of a fire breathing monster had existed for many years. It wasn't till 1910 that someone actually went to this mystery island with the intention of finding the illusive dragon. This was after Dutch sailors reported a sighting officially and a Dutch lieutenant called Steyn Van Hensbroek went on a hunting mission. After a few days, the lieutenant and his team were successful in killing one.

This specimen was measured at 6.9ft (21 meters long). Peter A Ouwens, who was the director of the zoological museum and the botanical gardens in Bogor, Java, took many photographs of the dragons. These photographs were used to create documented evidence of its existence. Further expeditions were taken; more dragons were killed for scientific study. It was concluded that the Komodo dragon was not able to breathe fire as the original rumours suggested.

The Komodo Dragon Home

The komodo dragon will dig holes that they can sleep in. They have to be big enough for the animal to fit into it comfortably. The holes are usually about 3-10 ft (1-3 meters) wide.

The dragon will generally choose to dig these burrows overlooking the sea to take advantage of the sea breeze. They clear all the vegetation from the area such as grass and plants and they also leave droppings near the entrance. This is so that they can remember where the burrows are. The komodo dragon will dig these holes using their strong claws.

The komodo dragon has no set home. They will use these holes to ambush prey such as deer. They may have several in different places and they do not necessarily favour one over another so they are not really komodo dragon homes. Instead they are more like shelters.

The Komodo Dragons Senses

Hearing	People used to think that the komodo dragon was deaf and it didn't appear to respond to sounds when being scientifically studied. But a lady who worked at the London Zoological Gardens didn't believe this. To prove that they could hear she trained a komodo dragon to recognise when food was out just by hearing the sound of her voice.
Vision	A komodo dragon can see 980 ft (300 meters). They are able to see moving objects better than still ones. They cannot see as well as night time as they can in the day.
Smell	Like many other reptiles the komodo dragon uses its tongue to smell. It may sound funny that the dragon smells with its tongue, but it's not in the same way that we use our noses. Instead it will stick out his tongue and the senses on it will pick up the same molecules in the air that our nostrils do. This way the dragon work out where an animal

	may be that it wants to eat.
Taste	The komodo dragon only has a few taste buds that are in the back of its throat.
Touch	The komodo dragon has very hard scaly skin but parts of it are more sensitive to touch than others. In these more sensitive parts they have sensory plaques which are connected to the dragon's nervous system and allow it to "feel." These sensory plaques are on the feet, lips, ears and chin. A komodo dragon can only feel touch in these four places on their body.

What do Komodo Dragons Eat?

Komodo Dragons are carnivores. This means they only eat meat. Their favourite meal is carrion. This is the meat of an animal that is already dead or dying.

Komodo dragons are good at ambushing unsuspecting animals. This means they will wait and hide for a long time until an animal it wants to eat (it's pray) comes close enough to attack. It will quickly charge and bite the throat of the animal with its many big sharp teeth. The komodo dragon will always prefer to attack animals that are already injured or poorly. This makes them easier to kill. The komodo dragon is very good at telling which animal will put up the least fight.

Its clever smelling tongue can also work out where other dead or dying animals are so they can take advantage and have an easy meal. They can "smell" a vulnerable animal up to 9.5 km (6 meters) away.

Their large tails are very strong and also help them catch their dinner. The komodo dragon can use it to knock down deer and pigs and then go for the throat.

Once the komodo dragon has made its kill it will tear the meat off with its teeth and swallow big chunks whole. If they are eating this way they tend to avoid parts of the animal that are vegetable based such as the intestines as the komodo dragon finds these parts harder to digest.

If the animal is smaller, such as a goat, it can eat it whole without chewing at all! The komodo dragon has flexible jaws which means they open really wide. It also has a stomach that expands enough to fit in a whole animal the size of a goat.

To help the food go down the komodo dragon doesn't have a glass of water. Instead it uses lots of red poisonous saliva. This red spit may have been where the rumours of fire breathing originated from.

Watching a komodo dragon eat a whole animal can look like quite a painful experience. They have been known to smash the carcass, half way down its throat, into a hard object like a tree to help it go down. The komodo dragon is a strong creature and this can sometimes cause the tree to fall down!

The komodo dragon will eat up to 80% of its own body weight of food in just one meal. That is the same as you eating a small pig in one go! As they eat so much at once they don't need to eat more than 12 times a year so at least they don't have to go through this ordeal every day!

Having such a large amount of food in their stomach can take a long time to digest. If it takes too long the meat will start to rot inside the dragon. It can get poisoned by the chemicals that are released as meat rots. The komodo dragon has a clever solution though. It will drag its heavy, full up body to the sun and sit in it for hours. The heat helps to speed up the process of digestion by breaking down the food while it's inside the stomach. It's a little bit like how we cook food only the komodo dragon does it after it has already been eaten!

What Eats The Komodo Dragon?

Nothing eats the komodo dragon. There are also no other big predators that eat the same prey as the komodo dragon. They are top of their food chain and control the eco system on which ever island they live.

The Komodo Dagon Family

The female komodo dragon lay eggs in the month of September. Each individual dragon will lay about 20 eggs. They leave them in special nesting holes and they do not look after them. The eggs stay in the holes, incubating for 7 months. It takes a very long time for the baby dragons to hatch themselves out of the eggs. When inside they are equipped with a special tooth called the "egg tooth" which is there just to do this job and falls out very soon after the dragon has hatched. This process is so tiring that they often will have to wait to rest and sleep after they have broken free from the egg. Then they will start to dig their way out of the nest their mother dug for them.

When they hatch they have to fend for themselves. They will hide in the trees until they are big enough..

One of the biggest threats to a baby komodo dragon is an adult komodo dragon. They are cannibals. That means they eat each other so the smaller and weaker of the species are vulnerable to the bigger, hungrier ones. To avoid being eaten by adults the young will roll around in excrement (poo) so that they smell bad. One theory is that the komodo dragon as a species is able to grow to a such big size because they eat each other!

When they are small they eat insects. It is useful that the time they hatch is the same time that most insects are around.

It takes 9 years for a baby komodo dragon to become a fully grown adult. They can live up to the age of 50.

As komodo dragons do not look after their young it is difficult to call them families. They are loner creatures who survive mainly on their own.

Komodo Dragons in Captivity

It has proved a difficult task to be able to keep komodo dragons in captivity. As soon as they were discovered people who owned zoos were very keen to have a real like dragon in their establishments. They attract a lot of attention and therefore a lot of visitors which means money to a zoo owner. However, the process has not been simple.

In 1934 the National Zoo in Washington had the first komodo dragon on show. As expected it was very popular but it only lived for two years. The average amount of time a komodo dragon was able to live in captivity was used to be just 5 years. They are susceptible to many diseases and infections and have had difficulty reproducing in captive conditions.

Studies have been undertaken since though that has given people more understanding of komodo dragons. This has meant that nowadays komodo dragons can live relatively well in captivity.

They have been observed "playing" with objects provided such as cans, rings, shoes. Other animals such as our family dogs often do this to find food or play at finding it. What is interesting about komodo dragons though is they do that seem to play just for the sake of it, for fun!

Komodo dragons have also been known to form "relationships" with humans while in captivity. They have the ability to learn how distinguish between different people and show this by displaying different reactions.

Why Are Komodo Dragons Vulnerable?

Komodo dragons are classified as "vulnerable" on the IUCN red list. This list is an extensive record of animals and plants and categorises them based on the possibility of extinction.

Classification	Examples of animals
Extinct	Dinosaurs
	Dodo
	Elephant Bird
Extinct in the Wild	Barbary Lion
	Hawaiian Crow
	Wyoming Toad
Critically Endangered	Amur leopard,
	Brown spider monkey
	Southern bluefin tuna
Endangered	Asiatic lion,
	Blue whale
	Common chimpanzee
Vulnerable	**Komodo Dragon**
	Cheetah
	Galapagos Tortoise
Near Threatened	Mountain zebra
	Polar bear
	Red panda
Threatened	Emperor penguin
	Jaguar
	Leopard
Least Concern	Baboon
	Bald eagle
	Brown bear

Being vulnerable means that there is a relatively high chance that the komodo dragon will become extinct if their situation doesn't change. When an animal is extinct it means there are no more of that species alive anywhere in the world. As the table above shows examples of extinct animals include dinosaurs.

What are the threats to the survival of the komodo dragon?

- There are roughly 4.000 komodo dragons in the wild but possibly only 350 females who are able to have babies.
- Volcano activity
- Fire
- Earthquakes
- Habitat loss (where they live being destroyed by natural causes or by humans)
- The komodo dragons prey (what they hunt and eat) being killed and taken by humans
- Humans killing komodo dragons illegally to take their skin for leather or killing for sport.

To address these issues humans have:

- Made poachers (people who kill animals in the wild for money) aware and prosecuted those who are caught killing komodo dragons.
- Tried to stop human activity affecting the natural habitat of the komodo dragon.
- Created the Komodo National Park in 1980. In later years the Wae Wuul and Wolo Tado Komodo Dragon reserves were opened. These places now cover all the islands where the komodo dragons live and aim to ensure that conditions are right to guarantee the continued survival of the species. People work very hard to make sure that they have everything they need to live and to reproduce within these parks.

- Work hard at ensuring komodo dragons do well in captivity. To do this people have to put a lot of time and money into the study of the dragons and aim to make the conditions perfect to help the dragons have babies.

Sadly the komodo dragon is already gone from one of the islands it once thrived. In 1975 the last ever komodo dragon was seen on the Indonesian island of Pedar. This shows how vulnerable the species is and without the intervention of the national parks, they may already be extinct in the wild.

When Komodo Dragons Attack

Date of attack	Wild or captive Dragon?	What happened in Attack	Result of Attack
April 2013	Wild	A komodo dragon bit into an 83 year old woman's hand. She kicked its front leg and then shouted for help.	The woman's hand was paralysed (wouldn't move) but has now recovered. She needed 35 stitches.
2007	wild	A German boy of 8 was ambushed and attacked while visiting the Komodo Dragon National Park.	Sadly the komodo dragon killed the boy.
2001	Captivity	A man, who was Sharon Stones husband was attacked when he was invited into an enclosure to meet some "tame" komodo dragons.	He needed surgery to put his big toe back on his foot and reattach the tendons.
1974	Wild	Baron Rudolf von Reding Biberegg was a European tourist visiting the Komodo Dragon National Park. He fell and injured his knee. He went to look for help but went missing	The only things that were found were a hat, camera, and blood on a stone.

| | | and it is assumed he was killed by a komodo dragon. | |

Other attacks have taken place throughout the years, as komodo dragons and humans come into contact unfortunately casualties are inevitable.

Could I keep a Komodo Dragon as a Pet?

No! The people who live on the islands where the komodo dragons live have to respect them, to understand them and to let them be. Our ways of life do not mix. The inhabitants who share their island with the dragon even have to have their homes on stilts, to keep the dragons out of their houses.

The closest a human will really get to a komodo dragon is by forming a relationship in captivity. This is only superficial though; a komodo dragon could not be stroked or cuddled. They are too big, powerful and hungry to be kept as pets.

As it has proven to be difficult to keep them alive in captivity and the very fact t they are on the "vulnerable" list shows that despite being so strong and deadly they are in fact very delicate creatures that would not adapt well to a human home and neither would the humans, who would probably a much shorter life expectancy.

Author Page

Lisa Barry was born Lisa Thomas in 1982, she grew up in Gloucester, England and moved to Wales at the age of 19 to become a primary school teacher. It was here she met her future husband. Lisa has had a varied career working with children and young people aged from 3 to19 years old. It was only after her second child was born though that she discovered a real love of writing. With her children for inspiration she is now embarking on an exciting and rewarding new career proving that life is always full of surprises.

Read More Amazing Animal Books

Purchase at Amazon.com

Website http://AmazingAnimalBooks.com

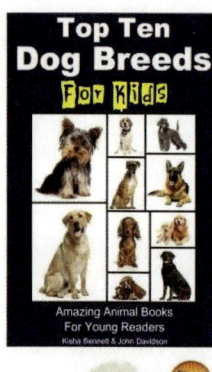

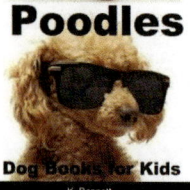

Our books are available at

1. Amazon.com
2. Barnes and Noble
3. Itunes
4. Kobo
5. Smashwords
6. Google Play Books

Download Free Books!

http://MendonCottageBooks.com

Publisher

JD-Biz Corp

P O Box 374

Mendon, Utah 84325

http://www.jd-biz.com/

Printed in Great Britain
by Amazon